Explore and Draw
SPACECRAFTS

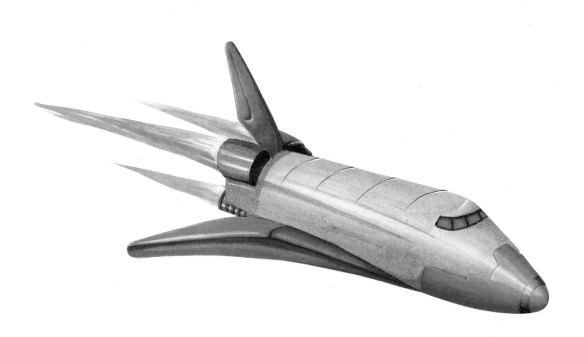

Ann Becker

www.rourkepublishing.com

Editor: Penny Dowdy
Art Direction: Tarang Saggar (Q2AMedia)
Designer: Neha Kaul (Q2AMedia)
Picture researcher: Jim Mathew (Q2AMedia)
Picture credits:
t=top b=bottom c=centre l=left r=right

Cover: NASA.
Insides: NASA: 6, NASA: 7, Neo Edmund/Shutterstock: 10,
James Steidl/Shutterstock: 11, PhotosCom/123rf: 14, NASA: 15, NASA: 18, NASA: 19.
Q2AMedia Art Bank: Cover, Title Page, 4, 5, 8, 9, 12, 13, 16, 17, 20, 21.

Library of Congress Cataloging-in-Publication Data
Becker, Ann, 1965 Oct. 6-
Spacecrafts : explore and draw / Ann Becker.
p. cm. – (Explore and draw)
Includes index.
ISBN 978-1-60694-352-6 (hard cover)
ISBN 978-1-60694-836-1 (soft cover)
1. Space vehicles in art–Juvenile literature. 2. Drawing–Technique–Juvenile literature.
I. Title. II. Title: Explore and draw.
NC825.S58B43 2009
743'.896294–dc22
2009021614

Printed in the USA
CG/CG

www.rourkepublishing.com - rourke@rourkepublishing.com
Post Office Box 643328 Vero Beach, Florida 32964

CONTENTS

TECHNIQUE

Before you draw spacecraft of the past or future, let's talk about **line**. Of course you use lines to draw your image. But certain lines do more than that.

1

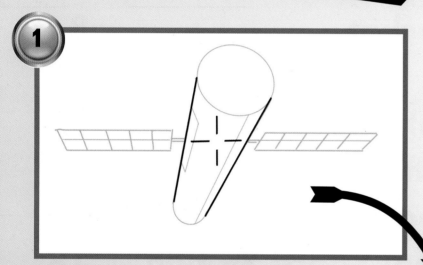

Leading lines are lines that move your eye to the most interesting part of the drawing.

2

Implied lines might be in the background, or on less important parts of the picture. But the implied lines still point to the interesting parts of your drawing.

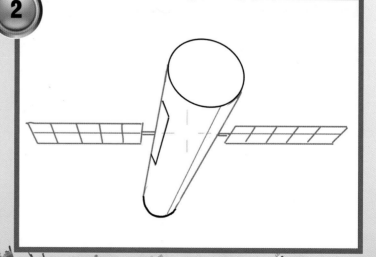

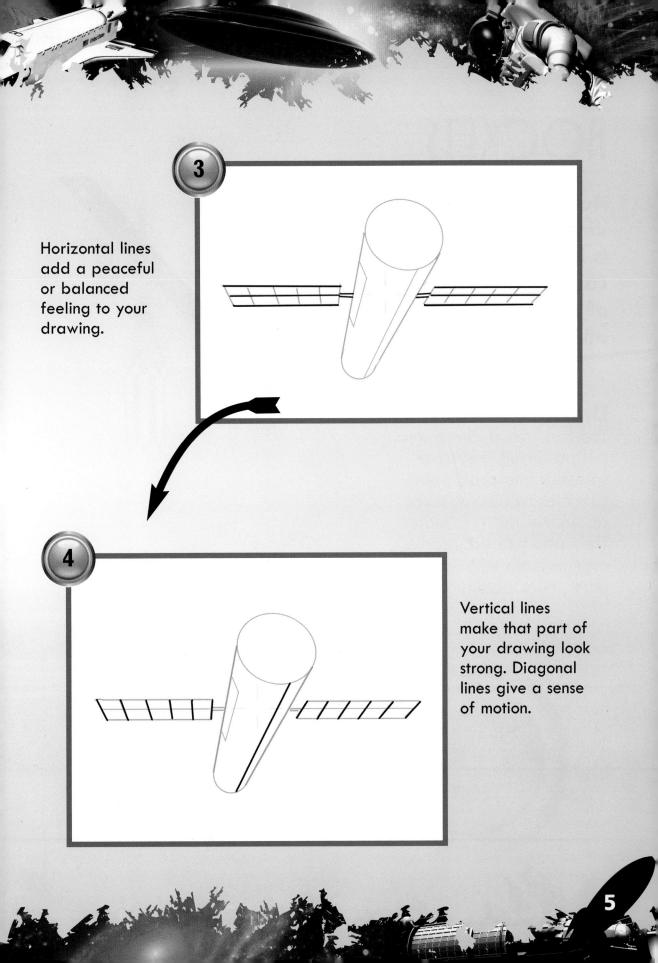

3

Horizontal lines add a peaceful or balanced feeling to your drawing.

4

Vertical lines make that part of your drawing look strong. Diagonal lines give a sense of motion.

ROCKETS

Humans have created many different kinds of rockets. It all depends on what is being lifted into space, and how far. Each rocket carries a **payload**. Some of the rockets send **satellites**, while others send astronauts.

Unmanned Rockets

The first rockets were small, but powerful! They sent satellites into orbit. These satellites helped us learn about the Earth's climate. They also helped people communicate with each other more quickly.

This rocket was part of NASA's *Mercury* rocket program.

This is a landing module that NASA used in the *Apollo* program.

Early Manned Space Programs

American scientists wanted to send people into orbit, and land on the Moon. *Mercury* astronauts used a small rocket. They stayed in space for about a day. *Gemini* astronauts reached a higher orbit. The *Apollo* program used the most powerful rocket built — the *Saturn V*. It carried the astronauts all the way to the Moon. Humans had finally walked on another world!

Staging Rockets

How can a rocket get someone all the way to the Moon? It has to be done in **stages**. The rocket has different sections that carry fuel. The lowest section burns all its fuel, and then drops off of the rocket. Then the next section burns its fuel. This way, the rocket gets lighter each time. Little by little, the astronauts get pushed all the way to the Moon.

DRAW A ROCKET

Most of a rocket is used to hold fuel. As each stage of fuel is used up, that stage can fall away from the rocket.

1 These lines are the start of the rocket. The lines are nearly vertical. The rocket looks powerful!

2 Finish the outline of the main rocket.

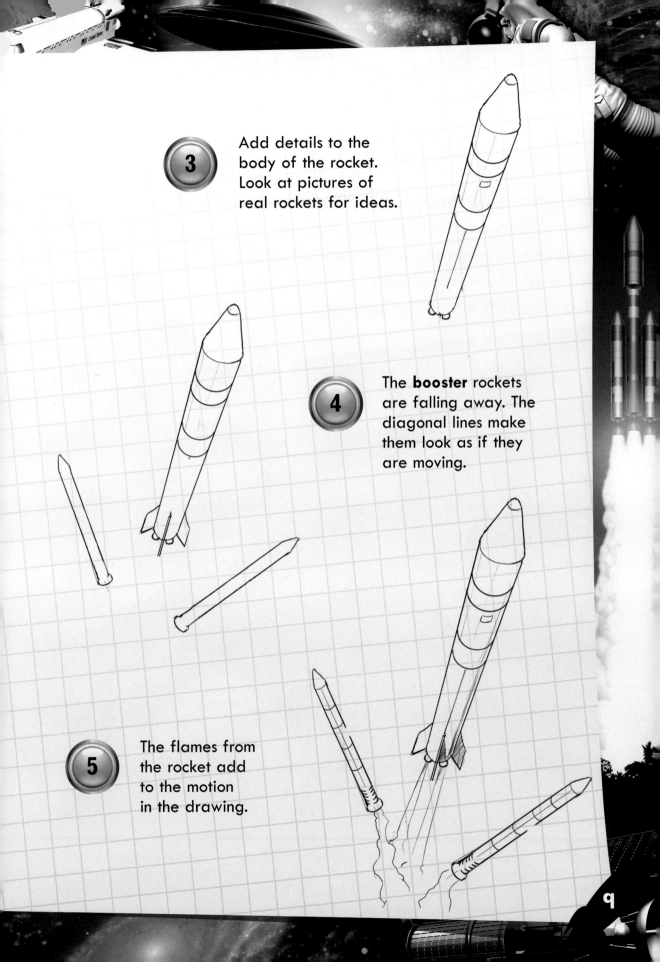

3 Add details to the body of the rocket. Look at pictures of real rockets for ideas.

4 The **booster** rockets are falling away. The diagonal lines make them look as if they are moving.

5 The flames from the rocket add to the motion in the drawing.

SATELLITES

Satellites help people understand their world. From orbit, a satellite can help scientists track a hurricane. Someone in Tokyo can call a friend in New York City. Other satellites let a country secretly spy on its neighbor.

Sputnik

In 1957, the world changed forever. That year, the Soviet Union was the first to put a satellite into orbit around the Earth. *Sputnik* studied the **atmosphere** for about three months. Its success launched the Space Race. Scientists in the United States worked frantically to catch up.

Spy Satellites

Satellites are also very useful for studying other countries up close. From orbit, cameras can photograph buildings, missiles, and just about anything else. As you might imagine, the technology in these satellites is top secret!

Satellites have solar panels to collect energy from the Sun.

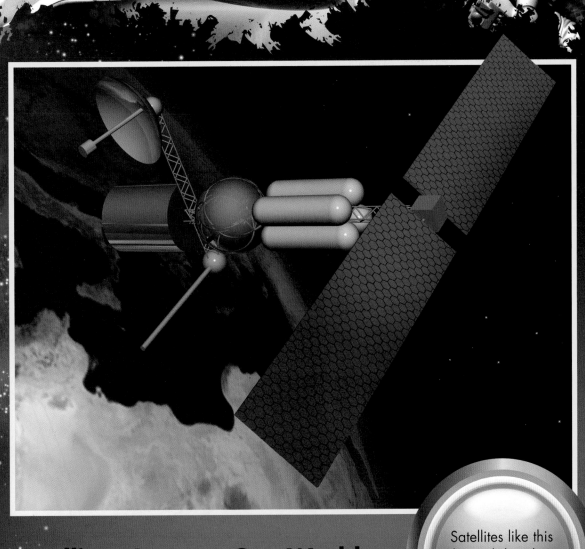

Satellites like this have dishes that collect signals from Earth.

Satellites Connect Our World

It's hard to think of our lives without television, the **Internet,** and long distance phone calls. Orbiting satellites have helped improve all these things. People living in **remote** areas can access their favorite websites. You can see the Olympic games as they're happening. Have you ever used a GPS device? Hundreds of satellites help you figure out how to get from here to there. These machines have really brought some wonders to our modern world!

DRAW A SATELLITE

A satellite orbits around Earth in space.

1 Start with the lines on the outside of the satellite.

2 Add the curves to the body of the satellite. The lines look like a target. They draw your eye to the top of the satellite.

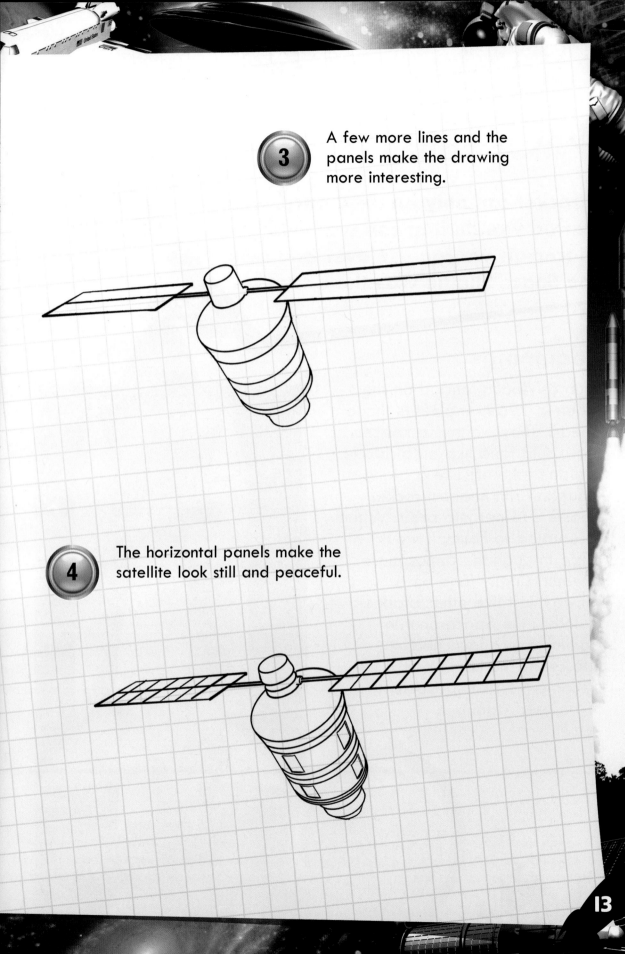

3 A few more lines and the panels make the drawing more interesting.

4 The horizontal panels make the satellite look still and peaceful.

SPACE SHUTTLE

A rocket can only be used once. Engineers started wondering: can we build a spacecraft we can use over and over? The Space Shuttle was the answer.

Beginnings

Even as *Apollo* landed on the Moon in 1969, engineers thought ahead. They wanted a spacecraft that could land like an airplane. It didn't take off like a plane, though. It still needed rocket boosters to get into orbit. When it returned to Earth, it would glide through the atmosphere. It would finally land on a runway, just like other planes. In 1981, the Space Shuttle *Columbia* was launched into orbit! The next year, it became the first spacecraft to be used again.

A Space Shuttle needs three huge fuel tanks and rockets to get it into space.

14

Space Shuttle Missions

The six shuttles have been the workhorses of the space program. They have placed satellites into orbit, including the Hubble Space Telescope. They are also used to retrieve and repair satellites. Science experiments that need **zero gravity** have been done on the shuttles. They also bring crucial supplies and parts to the International **Space Station**. For all that work, they've been worth every penny!

NASA moves the shuttle around the country by flying it on the back of a jet plane.

DRAW A SPACE SHUTTLE

The Space Shuttle looks a lot like an airplane, but the body and wings are different.

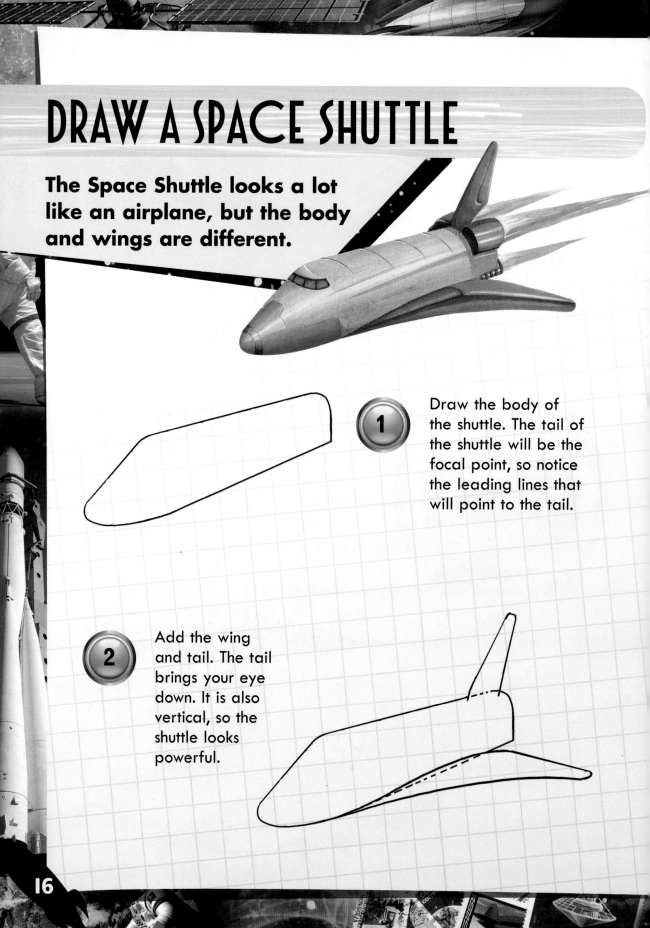

1 Draw the body of the shuttle. The tail of the shuttle will be the focal point, so notice the leading lines that will point to the tail.

2 Add the wing and tail. The tail brings your eye down. It is also vertical, so the shuttle looks powerful.

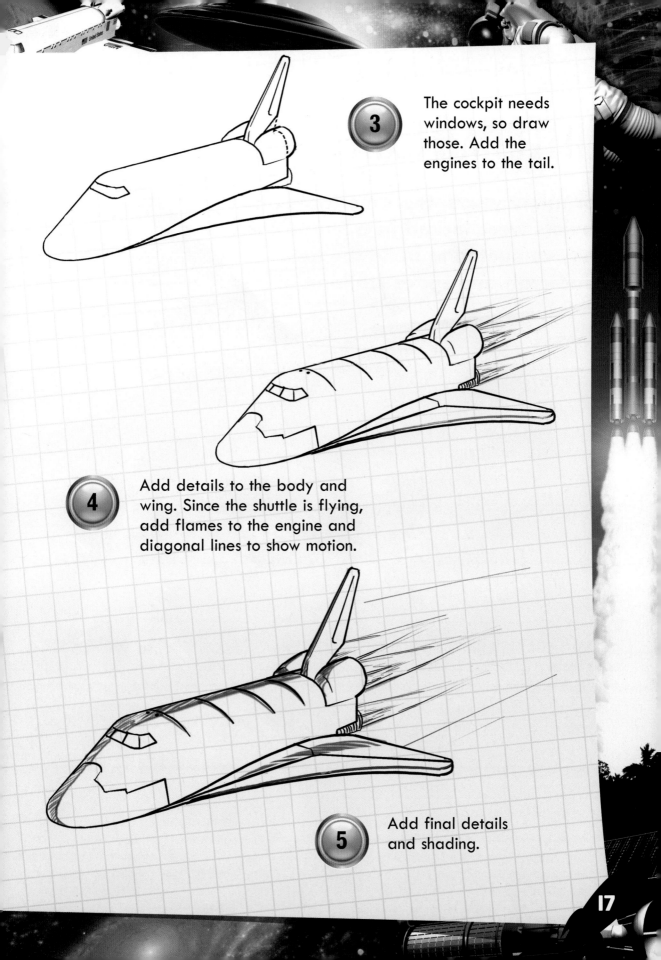

3 The cockpit needs windows, so draw those. Add the engines to the tail.

4 Add details to the body and wing. Since the shuttle is flying, add flames to the engine and diagonal lines to show motion.

5 Add final details and shading.

INTERNATIONAL SPACE STATION

For many years, the Americans and Soviets were locked in a Space Race. They competed to build the best spacecraft and space stations.

Planning the ISS

Keeping up with the competition was very expensive. So, both nations agreed to join in building the International Space Station. It was a big step towards peace between the two countries.

The Americans and Soviets weren't alone in designing the station. Japan, Canada, and eleven European countries joined them. Every country has **contributed** in some way: supplies, astronauts, scientists, whatever was needed. It was truly international!

The Space Shuttle docks with the ISS in order to bring the astronauts materials.

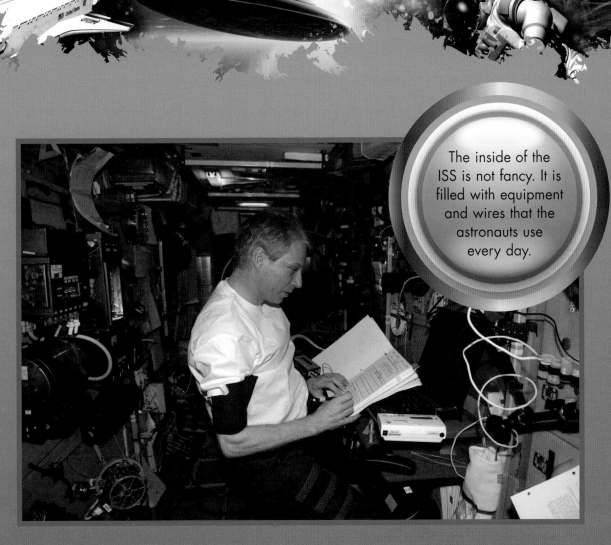

The inside of the ISS is not fancy. It is filled with equipment and wires that the astronauts use every day.

Modular Structure

The ISS was designed as **modules** that fit together. That way it could be put together a piece at a time. It has a laboratory for research. Engineers also created modules that control different systems, like heating and oxygen. It also has living quarters for people to live there permanently. In fact, the station has had someone living on it every day since 2000!

Research on the ISS

The ISS expanded human knowledge in many ways. Scientists studied how living in space affects the human body. They also learn how different gases and chemicals act in low gravity. Some research, like a cure for diseases, worked better in space. As they say: the sky's the limit!

DRAW THE SPACE STATION

The International Space Station lets scientists study space for long periods of time.

1 The ISS has a lot of rectangles. Sketch the rectangle that would cover the whole space station.

2 Divide the ISS down the middle. The drawing will now be two large sections connected by a narrow piece in between them.

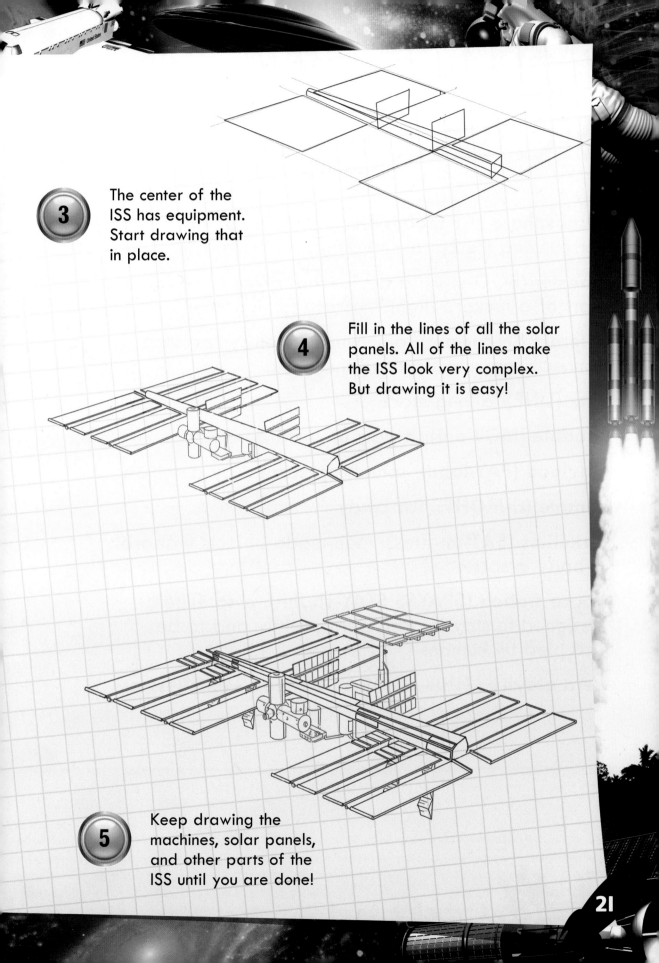

3 The center of the ISS has equipment. Start drawing that in place.

4 Fill in the lines of all the solar panels. All of the lines make the ISS look very complex. But drawing it is easy!

5 Keep drawing the machines, solar panels, and other parts of the ISS until you are done!

21

GLOSSARY

atmosphere (AT-muhss-fhir): the mass of air surrounding the Earth

booster (BOO-stur): a device that gives force for one part of a rocket's flight

Internet (IN-tur-net): a communication system that connects computers around the world

line (LINE): a long mark

module (MOJ-ool): a part of a structure

payload (PAY-lohd): something carried by a vehicle

remote (ri-MOHT): far away

satellites (SAT-uh-lites): man-made objects that orbit a body in space

space station (SPAYSS STAY-shuhn): a satellite designed to stay in orbit permanently and to be occupied by humans

zero gravity (ZIHR-oh GRAV-uh-tee): weightlessness

INDEX

WEBSITES

www.nasa.gov/home/index.html
Website devoted to all kinds of spacecraft, regardless of size, purpose, or the country in which it was developed.

www.esa.int/esaKIDSen/SEMDIIXJD1E_Liftoff_0.html
European Space Agency's website just for kids.

http://school.discoveryeducation.com/schooladventures/spacestation/
Discovery Education's website exploring the building of the International Space Station

drawsketch.about.com/od/kidsdrawingpages/Kids_Pages_Childrens
A list of different websites which tell how to draw a variety of things.

http://www.space.com/
A website containing news, photographs, videos, and features related to space and space exploration.

http://www.planetary.org/home/
The page of the Planetary Society, an organization devoted to inspiring space exploration.

About the Author
Ann Becker is an avid reader. Ann likes to read books, magazines, and even Internet articles. She hopes that someday she will get to go on a game show and put all of that reading to good use!

About the Illustrator
Maria Menon has been illustrating children's books for almost a decade. She loves making illustrations of animals, especially dragons and dinosaurs. She is fond of pets and has two dogs named Spot and Lara. When she is not busy illustrating, Maria spends her time watching animated movies.